Everything I Should Have Said

Sherri Eisenhardt

Presentation by *BookLeaf Publishing*

Web: www.bookleafpub.com

E-mail: info@bookleafpub.com

ISBN: 978-93-95890-32-8

First edition 2022

For Isaac, Emma, Ava, and Luci- may your shadows be bigger than mine, may you never settle, and may you know that I am always with you.

ACKNOWLEDGEMENT

Thank you Em, for pushing and making me circle back to passion time and time again, even when I was scared, even when the timing wasn't right. Thank you mom, for raising a fiery daughter. You are the bravest person I know. I'd be lost without you. Claude, you helped me transition into who I am now. Thank you for my new life. And Judy, for the unconditional love I found in true friendship.

PREFACE

I have stopped and started this book more times than I care to count. The more time that passes and the more I look back at each person that this book is meant to reach, I change. Most of these began as an apology that lead me to sacrificing parts of myself to keep the peace. Only now, I don't want peace. No more apologies. This is everything I should have said.

Goretti

When I said you couldn't leave a trail
Of hurt people behind you
While you try to find yourself again,

I meant it.

I wish you the torment of deep self reflection.
I wish everyone you burned
With your tongue heals.

I hope you are overwhelmed with forgiveness.

Navy Blue

So few things have buried their hands
In my soul

I'm hoping you'll be one of them

Fingernails would grow
Like roots

Hair braided underwater
Peace
By piece...
By peace...

Crossing over,
Folding space and time,
Walking thru

I'm hoping it'll be you,
Navy blue

Moonwalker

3

How absent of me
To be so close to you

Caught up on
Who shows up for who

I built this bridge to cross with you
Now you're gone
And I'm free to move

You gave excuses and I gave my best
It was never your fault
And I was obsessed

Tired of the war
Between my head and my chest
It's not a break but
Goodbye altogether

I hope you look for me
In everyone forever

Agent Reddish Yellow Burns
the Bridge

When you say things like

Every single me
In every single universe
Will spend all of forever
Looking for ways to love you more

How could my soul not shake?

When I say
That I'm just a bridge
That I'm strong enough for people
To need me only temporarily...
You tell me

In Wing Chun
We seek the bridge

Tell me I'm a maryter,
That I do it to myself.

It's easier if I hate you.
I change so fast.
I attempted to flee.

Your words
Not mine

May the bridges we burn
Light our way home.
May you be on it
Or spend lifetimes
Trying to find it

Sloppy Joe

I've never met anyone
So afraid of living

Sadness wrapped in glasses
With a restless beating heart

Tired of being the best of the only,
Finding comfort in self harm

Precipice meeting rock,
You shall not move

Juxtapose each moment,
Unquenchable

Love doesn't look like that

This is how the wolf cries boy
Just to bite the hand that feeds

I leave you just the way
I found you-

Alone.

Happy Birthday

Summer nights, 2009,
Relaxed when your eyes meet mine
Your smile somehow
Tries to tell me
What you're feeling right now

Looking back I realize this
With all of the signs I missed
And all of the time I took for granted
Just thought we were like this

And it makes me wish
I was wrong

Summer days, in a haze
Not knowing I feel the same
But we just couldn't so
Now it feels like letting go
Because my heart's not in it now
Not about sticking it out

God Is a Gemini

He's also a narcissist.

Vile
Putrid
And gluttonous.

Vain
Plain
And fallacious.

Ugly
Deceiving
And infectious.

Good.
Riddance.

It Goes Something Like This

First date

Drinks. Blanket fort. Cartoons.
Slow dancing in the hotel room.

Second date

Storm and rain.
At your mom's house.

Third date

Sleepover.
How are you so sweet so early in the morning?

Fourth date

Drinks and wings and
Conversations about deeper things.
I won't let myself have love that's
Less than gentle.

Fifth date

I'm not seeing anyone else.
Are you?

Sixth date
You're already walking on water..

Seventh date

I don't know where the time went
You've been here for a few days
and I could get used to this

It happened so fast
One minute I'm buying a toothbrush
And in the next breath
We're "in love"
And now I'm screaming
In a parking lot in Ahwatukee

I wanted to pause time there
dissect every emotion happening
In that moment

They say you should be here now...

It's been hours since I've come back to my
breath.

We did all that just to become strangers.

My Grief Has a Name

This was supposed to be my banner year

New job
New promotion
New raise
New me

Set like a proper dinner table

Enter him,
A brash ginger
Wearing a full beard,
Black glasses,
And a sideways smile
That an accent falls from

Z

There was nothing gentle
About his honesty
It was the kind that
Rubbed your face in the dirt
Before asking how much more
You can take

Without actually caring
About your answer

Pause for dramatics
Dialysis
Hospital
Dialysis
I don't feel good
Dialysis
Skipped coffee
Silence

No need for dialysis.
Or coffee.

I knew it was coming
But that didn't make it hurt less
Our days were numbered
I just thought we had more

I didn't share at first
I thought it made my grief unique,
That if it was quiet
It was more real
More special
I held onto it

This grief was a gift just for me.

And when I started to share,,
I was still alone

When the calls and texts
Start to slow
When the condolences
Decrescendo
When His voice
Starts to fade
when I struggle to
hear his accent in certain words
When it's hard to remember
The feel of his calloused hands
When the weight in my chest
Starts to feel a little less...
Heavy
When I start to breathe
for any reason other than
just surviving

Can I show grace in moving forward?
Can I hold someone else's hand?
Can I stay alone?
Can I meet the fact that
Some people will only be in my life
Because I had Z and I lost him?
Will I let someone else

Build a safe place for memories?
Will he see you as competition?

There is no room
For jealousy here.
My heart is big BIG
and I love to love.

Freeing Grace

When you left
I went to church

I hadn't spoken to God
In 3 years
And I still owe him one...
The lesson was on showing Grace
Which was kind of funny
Being that you disappeared

I had to ask myself
How that crow tastes

Now the flavor is
Going
Going
Gone

Atrilnguq Atghilnguq Atrituq

Finding your biological family
Feels a lot like
A sledgehammer
To the chest

First
The shock of it happening

Second
The pain of wishing it hadn't

All of the questions
None of the answers

Finding so many of them
Not knowing who they are

My mother called me a bloodhound
And I found that name...
Funny
Given that it's what I was looking for

All the words in the world
And none of them bring justice
To my emptiness

Kairoschlerosis

When I tried assign
Meaning to actions
In order to make sense
Of the inconsistency
I realized
I was burying myself
In nonsense

Feelings are funny like that;
Hope is the worst of them all
And has hurt me more
Than love ever could

It keeps you
Pushing
Breathing
Trying
And begging
Until you're reduced
To a shallow puddle
In comparison to
The depth you once were

It tires you
Wears you down

Breaks you
Into thousands of tiny pieces

They say diamonds are made under pressure
But not everything needs to be a gem

Sometimes

We need to take things
At face value
And refuse the tax

Linger

I disappear

In the way that
Your favorite scent
Will always be your favorite scent
Even though it's not quite the same each time

I disappear

In the way
That you smell the rain
Coming long before drops
Hit the roof

I disappear

In the way
That you keep
All those old keys on your key ring
Until someone new comes along
And passes judgement at the clutter

Shadow Alchemist

The way you pull strands of magic
From the universe
And fold them over your lap like laundry
Is enough to make anyone believe
In love

Draped in golds
The glow of your skin
In the sun
Is enough to make anyone remember what
freedom tastes like

Floating weightless
Effortless love envelopes across the skyline
And swallows the universe whole
It's enough to make anyone get lost following
you

Breathe in.

The fresh air in my nose
Has a cold crisp
That reminds me of our first kiss with winter
winds

Green eyes
Ever changing
Peels the power from a Siren's voice
As if it had fallen on deaf ears

Exhale.

The way you turn darkness into light
Is enough to make me wish
I was the one that
Discovered fire

Weaving everything from sadness
Until we no longer recognize
Our pain as an obstacle
But rather a witness
To pledge patience with the world
Even in it's not so beautiful moments

The way your fingertips dance across my face
As to say
You deserve a love that's gentle
Kind
Whole
Honest

The way I feel the safe in my skin
When I unpack the sadness
That doesn't belong to me
Rewind

Anemoia In the Slow Now

Cold feet in new evergreen sheets
The lump in my throat
Wants to break free
And spill out the words hung behind my teeth

My anger and sadness can pack a bite
In their shared suitcase
That we'll save for later

Blood pools in my mouth from biting my tongue

I swallow
It's both sweet and bitter roots
Trail down my chest

I throw the blanket over me
As if to say
"I'm not here now"
Though I'm not sure who
I'm trying to convince

I let the cold set in
It holds my heart like
It's glass AND gold

I do not move

My sadness is polished
Like a badge of honor
Hot breath for the finish

Worry seeps in
Like quiet smoke

What if I don't get better?
What if I do and I don't know what better is?

Rebellion

Everything I am
Stands in
Proud protest

Resilience

A scam perpetuated
To keep you filing down
Everything about yourself
Into an unrecognizable shell
In the name of strength

The Thing About Love

I am a hopeless romantic
But not in the classic sense

You see...

Hope creates attachment to an idea
So to say I'm hopeless
Is to say I'm brave
And to say I'm brave
Is to say I'm connected

Now

Love built on compromise
Is a love that will surely crumble
Weak foundation that was never set
Acceptance is love
The absence of requirement
Freedom
Still in my power
Watching them come and go
It's not to say it doesn't hurt,
Meets my chest hollow
Puts me in limbo in the space
Where I don't want to die

But sleep isn't quite enough
And I'm tired of waking up

I love myself
But
I don't love myself back

Reduce, Reuse, Recycle

On mornings like this
When I find myself wondering
How much of what you say to me
Has been said to others,
Is still being said to others,
The only thing that stops me
From be a sad jumbled mess now
Is realizing that
None of the compliments are genuine
And you recycle the same tired phrases
In hopes of luring someone else
Into you arms to fill the gaping hole
In your chest

How sad and incomplete you must be
To reduce yourself down
To catchphrases and fake tears
When you're afraid,
Not of losing me or anyone,
But afraid of losing the attention
And outside validation.
You hide behind blue eyes and a smile
But I can still smell
Your incompleteness in the dark

All the services you perform
All the words you use
All the kisses you give
All the gifts you bear
All the time you spend

And you're still weighed down by emptiness.

The Way We Move

An injustice and betrayal of trust
Wandering eyes and unquenchable lust
Tired words to many ears
Confirmation of all my fears

Pausing the moments and
Questioning what these feelings feed
Pulling myself up to
Set me free

A glance
At the mess you've made
At the wreckage left
At the root of need

A choice
To move through
To move on
To be still
To let the dust settle
To examine

Our hands touch
Words heavy in the air

Can we survive
And how is this fair?
Am I good enough and
What am I doing here?

A reclamation
A dedication and
A promise to never leave

Not to you but to me

Are You Lucid

Did they leave you here alone?
Yeah... They do that a lot.
Hi, I'm Sherri.
It's nice to meet you.
Lemme know if you need anything.

Did they leave you here alone?
Yeah, they do that. Sorry.
Hi, I'm Sherri.
You have a nice smile and sweet eyes.
Have tea with me?

Did they leave you alone here?
Yeah, they do that a lot.
Anyway... Hi, I'm Sherri.
Let me help you with that.
No I don't watch tv.
But I might make an exception.

Did they leave you here alone?
Yeah sorry, they do that a lot.
I'm Sherri.
I'll cut right to it then.
Your laugh...
Your smile...

Your train of thought...
Your eyes...
All of it.
Oh you play music?
That's cool.
No way! Saxophone? Me too!
Let me hear.
Stop being shy about it.
You give me chills.
This place doesn't deserve you.
I know you can do better.
Stop settling.
Escape. Now. While there's still time.

Sometimes I wonder what your hands feels like.
I bet you have soft lips.
Beards are great for neck snuggles.
I can't stop staring at you.

I'm not much of a hugger
But here's two.

Anyway...
Hi, I'm Sherri.
Nice to meet you.

www.ingramcontent.com/pod-product-compliance
Lightning Source LLC
LaVergne TN
LVHW010920200726
843509LV00013B/2010